Table of Contents

Introduction

A soft food diet, also called a bland diet, is made up of foods that are easy to digest. They're usually delicate in surface and low in fiber. The idea is to eat foods that are easy to swallow and that you don't require to chew much. You'll require to avoid spicy, fried, or gassy foods. A soft diet is made up of foods that are delicate and simple to bite and swallow. These foods may be cleaved, ground, mashed, pureed, and moist. You may need to follow this diet if you cjhave had certain types of medical procedure, such as head, neck, or stomach a medical procedure. You may also need to follow this diet if you have problems with your teeth or mouth that make it hard for you to chew or swallow food. Your dietitian will tell you how to follow this diet and what consistency of liquids you may have.

What is a soft food diet

Soft food diets consist of soft, easily absorbable foods and are endorsed to people who can't tolerate regularly textured or profoundly seasoned food sources. Healthcare providers commonly prescribed these diets to individual's with certain medical conditions or who are recovering from surgery. Soft food diets are used in numerous settings, including hospitals, long haul care facilities, and in the home. They're typically followed for short periods of a few days to a few weeks,

however some circumstances may require the diet to be followed for a longer period. Soft eats less carbs are often used to treat swallowing disorders, collectively known as dysphagia. Dysphagia is common in more established grown-ups and those with neurological issues and neurodegenerative infections. In 2002 the Academy of Nutrition and Dietetics published the National Dysphagia Diet (NDD), which incorporates several levels of dysphagia diets:

NDD Level 1 - Dysphagia-Puréed: uniform surface, pudding-like, requiring very little chewing capacity

NDD Level 2 - Dysphagia-Mechanically Altered: cohesive, moist, semisolid foods, requiring some biting

NDD Level 3 - Dysphagia-Advanced: delicate food sources that require more chewing capacity

Regular: all food sources allowed

In spite of the fact that the point of texture-modified diets is to reduce the risk of aspiration and pneumonia in individuals with dysphagia, current research proposes that modifying food surface may result in a worsened quality of life and undernutrition, featuring the need for more research. Likewise to dysphagia, delicate eating regimens are prescribed to people who have recently undergone mouth or jaw surgery that has impacted their capacity to chew. For example, people who have undergone wisdom teeth removal, major jaw surgery, or dental implant medical procedure may need to follow a soft diet to promote healing. Delicate diets are also utilized as temporary diets between full liquid or puréed diets and regular consumes less calories in people who have undergone stomach a medical procedure or are recovering from gastrointestinal illness to allow the digestive system to heal more successfully.

Additionally, soft diets can be prescribed to people who are too weak to consume ordinary foods, for example, those undergoing chemotherapy, as well as to people who have lost feeling in their face or mouth or can't handle their lips or tongue due to a stroke. Although soft food eats less carbs used in both the clinical and home setting can vary, most that are utilized in the short term are low in fiber and boring to ease digestibility and the solace of the person eating the diet. Keep in mind that some people have to be on delicate food diets for longer periods. In these cases, the eating routine may be higher in fiber and more flavorful than soft diets utilized in the short term.

Types of Soft Food Diets

There are two main types:

Mechanical soft diet. This includes foods that you don't need to chew as much. You'll eat things with different textures and thicknesses that are chopped, ground, mashed, or puréed. These foods are soft and tender, and you should be able to mash them with a fork.

Puréed soft diet. This is a bit more limited than a mechanical soft diet. You'll only eat foods that you don't need to chew at all. As the name implies, you can eat meals that include puréed foods or liquid foods. Liquids can be added to make swallowing

easier.

Who Should Eat a Soft Food Diet?

Your doctor will let you know if you need to eat this way. It can

be helpful in situations like these:

After surgery. It's common to follow a soft food diet while you

recover from certain operations. Your doctor could recommend

it if you've as of late had surgery on your:

- Mouth

- Tooth

- Head

- Neck

- Stomach

They could also tell you to follow the diet if you're getting radiation therapy to your head, neck, or stomach. Issues with digestion. A soft diet helps some people who have stomach related problems. The foods in the diet are simple to digest, so your digestive parcel will not have to function as hard to break them down. This sort of eating plan also features gentle foods that are less likely to disturb your stomach. Trouble chewing. The diet can help if you have an ongoing health condition that makes biting or gulping troublesome.

Foods to eat on a soft food diet

Soft diets are used when customary finished or highly prepared foods can't go on without serious consequences, which can happen for a number of reasons. Soft diets ought to not be mistook for puréed slims down. Although puréed foods are permitted on soft food diets, puréed abstains from food are totally unique. Overall, delicate diets should consist of foods that are soft, as well as easy to eat and digest.

Here are some instances of foods that can be enjoyed on most soft counts calories:

Vegetables: delicate cooked carrots, green beans, slashed cooked spinach, cooked zucchini without seeds, very much cooked broccoli florets, etc.

11

Organic products: cooked, peeled apples or fruit purée, bananas, avocado, peeled ripe peaches, cooked pears, puréed fruits, etc.

Eggs: cooked whole eggs or egg whites, egg salad

Dairy products: cottage cheese, yogurt, soft cheeses, pudding, frozen yogurt, etc. Lower fat dairy items are ordinarily suggested for individual's recovering from gastrointestinal medical procedure or illness.

Grains and starches: mashed potatoes, sweet potatoes, butternut squash, cooked oats like cream of wheat, delicate, moistened grains such as farro or grain, dampened pancakes, soft noodles, and so on

Meat, poultry, and fish: finely cleaved or ground moistened poultry, delicate tuna or chicken salad (without hacked crude vegetables or fruit like celery or apples), baked or seared fish, soft meatballs, soft tofu, and so forth

Soups: puréed or broth-based soups with delicate cooked vegetables

Miscellaneous: gravies, sauces, smooth nut margarines, unseeded jellies and jams

Drinks: water, tea, protein shakes, and smoothies

Keep in mind that there are various varieties of soft food diets, depending on the condition they're being used to treat. Some people with further limitations may not be able to tolerate certain foods for various reasons. Hence, it's always best to consult your medical care supplier or a registered dietitian on the off chance that you're following a delicate eating routine and have questions about what foods you're allowed to eat.

Foods to avoid

Many foods should be avoided when following a soft food diet. Hard to digest foods, as well as those that are tough to chew, should be restricted. Typically, spicy and very acidic foods are also off-limits.

The following foods are commonly restricted on soft diets:Vegetables: raw vegetables, deep-fried vegetables, vegetables with seeds or rinds

Fruits: fresh fruits (with some exceptions like avocados and bananas), fruits with peels and seeds, dried fruits, highly acidic fruits like lemons and limes

Dairy products: hard cheeses, cheeses with nuts or dried fruit in them, yogurt with added ingredients, such as chocolate or nuts

Grains and starches: hard crackers, chewy or crusty breads, high fiber breads and grains, such as seeded breads and shredded wheat, French fries, popcorn

Meat, poultry, and fish: tough cuts of meat, fried fish or poultry, whole cuts of meat or poultry, high fat processed meats, such as bacon, shellfish, soups or stews with tough chunks of meat

Fats: nuts, seeds, coconut flakes, crunchy nut butters

Miscellaneous: seeded jams or jellies, chewy candies

Spicy or irritating foods: hot peppers, tomato sauce, gas-promoting foods, such as cabbage and beans, tabasco sauce

Beverages: alcohol, caffeinated beverages may be restricted as well depending on the condition being treated

Note that your healthcare provider may recommend further restrictions depending on your medical condition. It's important to have a good understanding of the diet that's prescribed and your individual dietary needs.

Soft food diet meal and snack tip

Following any restrictive diet can be frustrating, especially when numerous solid foods like crude fruits and vegetables are off-limits. All things considered, there are many tasty supper and nibble options for those following delicate diets.

Here are some ideas for meals that can be eaten by people following delicate diets:

Breakfast thoughts

Fried eggs and sliced avocado

Cream of wheat topped with cooked peaches and creamy cashew spread

Crustless quiche made with eggs, goat cheese, minced spinach, and butternut squash

Yogurt parfait made with unsweetened yogurt, banana or canned peaches, seedless blueberry jam, and smooth almond margarine

Lunch ideas

- chicken or tuna salad made without vegetables

- chicken soup with soft noodles, cooked veggies, and

  small bits of tender, shredded chicken

- couscous, feta, and soft vegetable salad

- moist salmon burger with avocado

Supper thoughts

- meatloaf made with ground beef or tofu alongside

  squashed sweet potatoes

- broiled flounder with soft cooked beets and carrots or

  cheesy mashed potatoes

- soft chicken and rice with cooked green beans

- shepherds pie made with ground turkey

- In addition to meals, many individuals following a soft diet probably will need to include one or more snacks throughout the day.

- Some snack thoughts include:cottage cheese with cooked or soft canned fruit

- yogurt with cooked peeled apples and cinnamon

- vegetable and grain soup

- all around mixed smoothies made with protein powder, smooth nut margarine, and natural product

- egg salad made with mashed avocado

- damp pumpkin or banana bread with smooth almond spread

- puréed vegetable soups, such as butternut squash soup

- banana boats with smooth natural nut butter

It's vital that all suppers and snacks be as balanced as possible and include high protein foods, particularly for the individuals who have recently gone through surgery or have higher supplement needs, such as those with cancer.

15 Soft Foods to Eat After Having Your Wisdom Teeth Removed

Wisdom teeth are moreover known as third molars. They grow at the back of your gums and are typically the last teeth to emerge. Most people have four sagacity teeth, one in each back corner of their mouth. However, because there's little space at the back of your mouth, your wisdom teeth may develop at odd focuses or only not entirely emerge. These are called impacted wisdom teeth. Impacted wisdom teeth can cause a variety of problems. They may get infected, damage neighboring teeth, cause amassing or start to decay since they're hard to clean. To address these concerns, people often get their wisdom teeth removed. However, wisdom teeth don't need to be removed unless they cause problems. After you've had your wisdom teeth removed, it's very fundamental to ensure you're getting the right nutrition. A nutritious diet restricts the risk of complications, helps decrease swelling, provides food, and helps the wound retouching process. The foods you eat after surgery should be fragile and easy to chew. They should also have lots of supplements, minerals, energy, and protein to assist wound healing.

Here are 15 soft foods you should eat after having your wisdom teeth killed.

1. Blended soups

Blended soups, like tomato or pumpkin soup, are unprecedented to eat after you've had your wisdom teeth removed. They're easy to consume and don't contain bits that could irritate the area of surgery. In addition, soups are all things considered rich in vitamins and minerals. This ensures you meet the consistently nutrition ideas when you can't eat many whole normal items or vegetables. Blended soups can also keep you hydrated, which is very important after operation. It's astute to ensure your soups are either lukewarm or cold, in light of the fact that hot soups can cause irritation.

Also, make sure to blend vegetable-based soups as smooth as possible to avoid chunks.

2. Stocks

Like soups, broths are an excellent source of nourishment after dental surgery. Not simply are they delicious, they also contain a grouping of supplements and minerals. Also, broths are a mind blowing way to stay hydrated if you struggle to drink enough water. Bone broth is a sort of broth touted for its health benefits. It's a nutritious stock made by simmering animal bones and connective tissue. Although there are no direct focuses on the prosperity effects of bone broth, studies on the parts of bone stock propose it may have relieving benefits. Make sure to consume the stock either lukewarm or cold to avoid upsetting the wound.

3. Greek yogurt

Greek yogurt is a nutritious high-protein food you can appreciate after dental operation. It has a smooth and creamy texture that could help soothe and numb your mouth. Greek yogurt is rich in protein, vitamins, and minerals such as calcium and zinc. High-protein foods may aid the recovery process. Honestly, several studies have linked a low-protein diet to a slower recovery. Additionally, studies show that an good zinc intake may promote wound healing. Regardless, if your zinc status is already good, consuming additional zinc may provide no added benefits. That said, various zinc-rich foods such as steak and various meats are difficult to consume after dental surgery, so Greek yogurt can be a great elective.

4. Crushed potatoes

Potatoes are a root vegetable that can be prepared in many ways. Specifically, mashed potatoes can be a comforting food after you've had your wisdom teeth removed. They're rich in calories and supplements, both important for recovery. This is because people have slightly higher energy requirements after having surgery. Beat potatoes grant you to consume lots of nutrients and energy in just a few bites, which is great if you're struggling to eat enough food. Just make sure that your mashed potatoes are lukewarm or cold, as hot foods may exasperate the wound.

5. Scrambled eggs

Eggs are among the best food assortments to eat after having your understanding teeth out. They're a wellspring of high quality protein rich in vitamins and minerals. When it comes to buying eggs, try to find pasteurized or omega-3-improved varieties. Omega-3 fats may help wound healing. Scrambled eggs can be more straightforward to chew and swallow, differentiated and other egg preparations.

6. Applesauce

Apples are hard and crunchy, which isn't ideal after having your insight teeth wiped out. Eating applesauce is one way to increase your regular item intake while avoiding irritation. Regardless, organic product purée is usually made from puréed apples, which are ordinarily skinless and cored and this reduces their restorative content. This is because the skin contains various supplements, minerals, and fiber. Nevertheless, a skinless apple is a good source of vitamins like vitamin C. This supplement may help boost the immune system, which in turn may aid the wound repairing process.

7. Mashed bananas

Bananas are among the most popular regular items in the world. Their fragile texture makes them basic to chew and swallow after dental surgery. What's more, bananas are incredibly nutritious and give a wide grouping of vitamins and minerals, similar to potassium, vitamin B6, manganese, and folate. Crushing bananas can further unwind their texture to reduce the risk of trouble.

8. Banana ice cream

People often recommend eating ice cream when you're recovering from wisdom tooth operation. While the energy may have a diminishing effect on the wound, regular ice cream is ordinarily high in sugar and fat. Banana ice cream is a healthy and delicious locally built alternative to standard ice cream.

How to Make Banana Ice Cream

Ingredients

- 3–4 bananas, peeled

- a splash of milk (or almond or oat milk if you'd like a dairy-free alternative)

Directions

1. Place bananas in the freezer for 3–4 hours or overnight.

2. Cut frozen bananas into slices.

3. Place frozen bananas into a blender and add milk.

4. Blend until mixture has a thick, smooth consistency and enjoy.

9. Avocado

Avocados are a unique fruit. While most fruits are high in carbs, avocados are low in carbs but high in healthy fats. Their smooth, creamy texture makes them great for eating when you're recovering from having your wisdom teeth taken out. Avocados are very nutritious and a rich source of vitamin K, vitamin C, and potassium. One study in animals found that avocados may speed up the wound healing process. Although this research doesn't indicate whether avocados speed wound healing in humans, the findings are promising. While avocados are usually easy to eat, it may be easiest to consume whipped or mashed avocado during your recovery.

10. Smoothies

Smoothies are a great way to boost your nutrition when you can't eat a solid meal. They're easy to consume and highly versatile. You can adjust the ingredients in smoothies to suit your tastes and meet your nutrition goals. For example, smoothies with Greek yogurt or a scoop of protein powder can boost your protein intake significantly, which is important for recovery. Studies have shown that a low protein intake may impair the recovery process. Try adding some fruit and vegetables into the blender alongside your choice of protein. It's best to use fruit that's seedless, so you may want to avoid things like strawberries and blackberries.

11. Hummus

Hummus is a common dip in Middle Eastern cuisine that's become popular worldwide. It's a great source of healthy fats, vitamins, minerals and protein. This makes hummus an excellent food for someone who just had their wisdom teeth removed. You can make hummus by blending chickpeas, olive oil, tahini, lemon, and garlic in a food processor. Alternatively, you can purchase premade hummus from most supermarkets. Unfortunately, you may not be able to enjoy hummus with chips or pita bread because their crunchy texture may damage the wound. However, hummus is still delicious to eat by itself.

12. Cottage cheese

Cottage cheese is low in calories and packed with vitamins and minerals. It's soft and creamy, which makes it easy to chew and swallow as you're recovering from wisdom tooth surgery. Additionally, cottage cheese is packed with protein, which may aid wound recovery. Cottage cheese is also easy to incorporate into your diet. Try adding it to scrambled eggs or into your smoothies.

13. Instant oatmeal

Oats are among the most nutritious foods. They're filling and a good source of fiber, plus they contain vitamins and minerals. Oats do have a slightly chewy and sticky texture, so it's best to wait to consume them until at least 3 days after having your wisdom teeth removed. It's also best to opt for instant oatmeal because it's less chewy than other types, such as oatmeal made with steel cut oats. To avoid irritation, make sure the oats have cooled down before you eat them.

14. Mashed pumpkin

Mashed cooked pumpkin is great to eat after you've had your wisdom teeth removed. While sometimes referred to as a vegetable, it's actually a fruit. Its soft, mushy texture makes it easy to chew and swallow without causing irritation. What's more, pumpkin is rich in vitamins A, C, and E, as well as minerals like potassium. These vitamins may help promote immunity, which in turn may help the body recovver from wisdom tooth removal. However, make sure to let the pumpkin cool down so it won't irritate your wound.

15. Salmon

Salmon is one of the healthiest fish you can eat. It's also great to eat after dental surgery because it's soft and easy to chew. Salmon is a rich source of protein and healthy fats like omega-3 fatty acids. These fats may aid wound healing by reducing inflammation, especially if you already have low omega-3 fatty acid levels. Although inflammation is essential to the wound healing process, excess inflammation can hinder recovery if it lasts too long.

Foods to avoid

Several types of foods can irritate the wounds in your mouth as they're healing after surgery.

Here are some foods to avoid after wisdom tooth removal:

1. Spicy foods: may cause pain and irritation.

Crunchy and crumbly foods (like chips or cookies): may get lodged in the wound area and disrupt healing

Most grains and seeds: can also get lodged in the wound and disrupt healing

2. Chewy foods: can increase your risk of biting your cheek, lips, and tongue, especially soon after the surgery while your mouth is still numb

3. Alcohol: may irritate the wound or interact with any prescribed medication (it's best to avoid it entirely during the recovery period)

It's also important to avoid using a straw while you recover from wisdom tooth removal. Straws create suction in the mouth that increases the risk of developing a dry socket. A dry socket is a painful condition in which the clot protecting the area where the tooth was removed becomes dislodged. As a result, the underlying bones and nerves are exposed to air, which causes pain and delays healing.

Soft Food Diet Recipes

1. Heavenly Mashed Potatoes

INGREDIENTS

- 4 russet potatoes, peeled and cut into chunks

- ⅓ cup heavy cream

- ¼ cup (½ stick) unsalted butter

- 2 garlic cloves, minced

- ¼ cup cottage cheese, pureed

- 2 tablespoons chives, thinly sliced

- salt and pepper to taste

- optional garnish

- chives

- melted butter

INSTRUCTIONS

1. Place potatoes in a large pot and fill with water. Place over medium-high heat and bring to a boil.

2. Boil potatoes until fork tender, about 25 minutes.

3. While potatoes boil, place cream, butter and garlic in a small saucepan and simmer. Once mixture comes to a simmer, remove from heat.

4. Drain potatoes in a colander and return back to the pot. Lightly mash the potatoes and season with salt and pepper.

5. Pour cream mixture over the potatoes, a little at a time and mash the potatoes until all the cream mixture has been used and potatoes are smooth.

6. Stir in pureed cottage cheese and sliced chives and season with salt and pepper.

7. Top with remaining chives and melted butter, if desired. Serve warm.

2. Messy Spinach Mashed Potato Cups

Fixings

- 3 cups leftover crushed potatoes

- 2 large eggs

- 1 package frozen spinach, thawed and depleted thoroughly

- 1 tsp garlic powder

- 1 tsp salt

- ½ tsp black pepper

- ¾ cup destroyed cheese of your choice, in addition to extra for beating

Guidelines

- Preheat broiler to 375F.

- Spray a muffin tin with cooking shower and set aside.

- Make sure that all of the extra water has been drained out of the thawed spinach. Mix all ingredients in a bowl until well combined.

- Scoop mixture into muffin cups and top with extra cheese.

- Prepare for around 30 minutes or until the sides of the cups turn light brown.

3. Flavored Sweetpotato Cauliflower Mash

Fixings

- 3 pounds California Sweetpotatoes, peeled and chopped into 1" chunks (around 3 large)

- 1 1/2 pounds cauliflower florets (from 1 large head)

- 1/4 cup milk

- 1/2 cup plain Greek yogurt

- 2 teaspoons cinnamon

- 1/4 teaspoon allspice

- 1/4 teaspoon nutmeg

- 2 tablespoons brown sugar

- 1 1/4 teaspoons kosher salt

- Fresh chives, chopped (optional)

Bearings

Fill a huge pot with 1-2 inches of water. Using a steam bin or large colander, steam potato and cauliflower until very soft, around 15 to 20 minutes, throwing infrequently.

Move vegetables to a large bowl, or stand blender if you have one. Add remaining fixings: milk, Greek yogurt, cinnamon, allspice, nutmeg, earthy colored sugar and salt. Mix everything together using a hand (or stand) mixer until wanted consistency is came to. If the mash is too thick, add more milk on a case by case basis. Garnish with chives, extra cinnamon and/or earthy colored sugar if desired.

4. Spice and Garlic Mashed Potatoes

Ingredients

- 1 head garlic, small

- 6 potatoes, medium

- salt to taste

- 50ml/1/4 cup whole milk, hot

- 100g/1/2 cup unsalted butter

- 1-2 tbsp parsley

- 1-2 tbsp dill

Directions

Preheat the oven to 200C/400F. Cut the top off the head of garlic to expose the cloves, wrap in aluminum foil and prepare for 45-50 minutes until the cloves are very soft. Cool.

Boil the stripped and quartered potatoes in salted water until very tender. While the potatoes are cooking, crush the garlic cloves out of their peels, they should pop out easily and mash them with a fork in a small bowl. Set aside.

Drain the potatoes and steam dry them to get rid of the excess of water. Return them to the pot and add hot milk, begin crushing with a potato masher until mostly smooth, then, at that point, add spread and keep mashing. Begin by stirring in ½ of the crushed roasted garlic, slowly increase the garlic quantity according to taste, then, at that point, pound until smooth and

most lumps are broken, season with salt to taste. Add the fresh

herbs and fold in with a spatula. Serve piping hot with a bit

more spread if desired.

5. Potato Pancakes

Fixings

- 3 cups mashed potatoes

- 2 large eggs

- 1/2 cup flour

- 1/2 cup shredded cheddar cheese

- 1 teaspoon dried parsley

- salt and pepper to taste

- oil for searing

Instructions

Preheat a large frying pan or griddle to medium heat.

In the event that your potatoes are cold from the refrigerator, I recommend warming them up somewhat and giving them a second mash or beating with a electric mixer so they're more straightforward to work with.

In a huge bowl add the mashed potatoes, eggs, flour, cheese, parsley, salt and pepper.

Stir the ingredients together.

Grease the griddle/skillet lightly.

Form the dough into patties about ¼ cup of batter each. Flatten the patty between your palms.

Fry on the one side until golden (around 3-5 minutes), then flip

and fry on the second side until golden.

6. Irish Colcannon

Fixings

- 3 lbs reddish brown potatoes peeled and chopped

- 5 Tbsp margarine divided, plus more for serving

  whenever wanted

- 8 cups chopped kale, around 1 large bunch (remove the

  tough stems first)

- 1 cup half-and-half or buttermilk

- 1/2 tsp salt or, to taste

- 4 tsp horseradish sauce

Instructions

Bring a huge pot of water to a boil, add the chopped potatoes, and simmer for about 10-15 minutes until the potatoes are very tender. (The tip of a sharp blade should slide in easily.)

Drain the potatoes and set them aside.

In the same pot, melt 2 Tbsp of butter, and sautee the chopped kale over low-medium heat for 5-10 minutes until soft.

Take off the hotness, add the potatoes back to the pot along with the rest of the margarine, half-and-half, salt, and horseradish sauce. Pound together with a potato masher until all the ingredients are fully joined.

Adjust seasonings to taste, and serve with more butter if desired.

7. Stacked crushed potato skillet

Ingredients

- 6 small potatoes

- 1 1/2 Tbsp vegetable or canola oil, DIVIDED

- 1 tsp kosher salt

- 4 slices bacon, cooked and crumbled

- 1 1/2 cups shredded cheddar cheese

- 1 Tbsp butter

- Salt and Pepper

- Sour Cream, for embellish

- Sliced green onions, for embellish

Guidelines

Wash your potatoes, if necessary, and poke a couple of times with a knife. Place on to a microwave safe plate and microwave until mostly cooked, around 10 minutes. (You can also boil them to this point, if you like. Allow to dry before placing in skillet).

Preheat stove to 425° Place 1 Tbsp. oil in lower part of skillet and brush a bit up the side. Sprinkle the bottom of the pan with 1 tsp. of kosher salt. Place pre-cooked potatoes in to skillet and place in the broiler for about 10 minutes, or until very delicate. Eliminate skillet from oven and, using a potato masher, crush each of the potatoes, until quite thin. Place a small pat of butter on top of each potato and season with salt and pepper. Brush the outside of the potatoes with the stay 1/2 Tbsp. of oil. Return to the stove for another 5-10 minutes or so, or until they crisp up. Eliminate from stove again and top with crumbled bacon and shredded cheese. Return to the oven until the cheddar is melted and effervescent.

Embellish with spots of sour cream and sliced green onion.

8. Cheesy mashed potato casserole

Ingredients

- 5 lb potatoes peeled and cubed

- 1 c sour cream

- 1/2 c butter

- 8 oz cream cheese cubed

- 1/2 c milk

- 2 tsp garlic salt

- pepper to taste

- 12 slices bacon cooked, chopped, and divided

- 2 c cheddar cheese divided

- 1/2 c parmesan cheese

- green onions for garnish

Instructions

Peel and cube potatoes.

Place in pot and add water until just covering potatoes. Bring to boil. Once boiling, reduce to a simmer and cook for 18-20 minutes.

Drain water and mash potatoes using a masher or spoon. Add sour cream, butter, cream cheese and milk until well combined.

Add salt and pepper. Fold in ½ the bacon, 1 cup cheddar cheese, and parmesan cheese. Mix well.

Spoon into lightly greased 9×13 pan. Top with remaining cheddar cheese and the rest of the bacon.

Bake at 350 for 20-25 minutes. Garnish with green onions and ENJOY!

9. High protein egg scramble with quinoa

Ingredients

- 2 large eggs, slightly beaten

- 2 Tbsp. shredded mozzarella (or Parmesan)

- 1 cup fresh spinach, roughly chopped

- 1 Tbsp. Extra Virgin Olive Oil

- 2 cloves garlic, chopped

- 1/4 cup cooked quinoa

- pinch salt and pepper

- 2 Tbsp. microgreens or fresh basil (optional)

Instructions

Over medium heat, heat olive oil and garlic in small frying pan.

Whisk eggs in a small bowl and pour into the pan.

Once eggs starts to cook add in the spinach, cheese and quinoa.

Mix together. Season with salt and pepper. Garish with more cheese and any fresh herbs you prefer.

10. Italian egg scramble

Ingredients

- 2 red potatoes, diced
- 1 Tbsp olive oil
- 1/8 tsp garlic powder
- 1/8 tsp dried basil

- 1/8 tsp dried oregano

- 2 Tbsp butter

- 1/4 cup red onion, diced

- 5 eggs

- 2 tomatoes, diced

- 2 cups baby spinach

- 2 Tbsp jullienned fresh basil

- 1/4 cup crumbed feta cheese

Instructions

Preheat the oven to 400 degrees F. Toss the diced potatoes with the olive oil, garlic powder, basil and oregano. Spread onto a baking sheet and roast until fork tender, about 20-30 minutes.

Once the potatoes are done, heat a large skillet on medium-low.

Add the butter and red onion. Cook for 3-4 minutes until the onion is soft. Add the five eggs and gently push until almost cooked through. Add the roasted potatoes, tomatoes and baby spinach and fold in until the eggs are cooked through.

Remove from heat and add the basil and feta before serving.

11. Baked egg potato bowls

Ingredients

- 6 large potatoes

- 6 eggs

- about 3 tbsp olive oil

- 5 oz (150 grams) shredded or cubed cheese (any kind you like; more kinds can be combined)

- 2 stalks green onions

- 9 oz (250 grams) bacon, cubed and fried

- salt

- pepper

- red pepper flakes

Instructions

Preheat the oven to 400 °F (200 °C).

Wash the whole potatoes under running water thoroughly.

Bake the potatoes until they are cooked through and soft inside

(it will take about 40 minutes).

Remove the potatoes from the oven and let them cool to the temperature that will allow you to handle them with your hands.

Decrease the oven temperature to 350 °F (175 °C).

Slice a layer off the top of each potato. Using a spoon, gently scoop out insides, leaving a thin layer of potato against the skin and avoiding puncturing the bottom. Reserve the scooped potato for another use.

Brush the inside of each potato with the olive oil.

Add a little salt, pepper and red pepper flakes.

Sprinkle a layer of bacon, thin slices of green onions and some shredded cheese into each potato. Fill each potato about ½ full.

Crack one egg into each potato.

Sprinkle with a little more bacon, onion slices and cheese. Then top with more salt, pepper and red pepper flakes.

Place the potatoes on a baking sheet and cook for about 20 minutes.Egg whites should be set and yolks soft.

12. Cheesy rice balls

INGREDIENTS

- Arancini

- 1 recipe of my Super Creamy Parmesan Risotto

- 1.5 Cups Grated Mozzarella

- 1 Cup Grated Parmesan

- 1 Egg

- 2 tbsp finely chopped parsley

- ½ cup plain flour

- Salt

- Black pepper

- Breading and Frying

- 2 eggs

- 2 cups panko breadcrumbs

- 1 48 oz bottle of Vegetable Oil

- Dips

- Marinara

- Chipotle Aioli

- Garnish

- Chopped parsley

- Lemon Zest

- Lemon wedges

INSTRUCTIONS

Combine COOLED risotto, Mozzarella cheese, Parmesan cheese, egg and parsley in a bowl just until everything is mixed through. If the mixture is not sticking together just add in some breadcrumbs one tablespoon at a time.

Place some parchment paper on a medium size baking sheet and start scooping the risotto mixture onto the baking sheet so that you have nice balls. You may need to roll the balls a bit in your hands to keep them from sticking to your hands. I find that scooping them with anice cream scoop is the most efficient!

Pour the whole container of oil into your pan. Start heating it up to 350 degrees or until a few bread crumbs turn brown. DO NOT **GET RID OF THE BOTTLE.**

Season the flour, egg and Panko breadcrumbs with salt and pepper.

Roll the balls in the flour first, then eggs then breadcrumbs.

Place onto the same sheet pan in preparation to fry.

Prepare a large plate covered with a clean dish towel or a few layers of paper towels to use after the arancini are fried.

Once you have tested the oil and ensured it is hot enough, place the balls in carefully and allow to fry until golden brown each side will take about 2 minutes although the second side may

very well go faster.

Place the arancini onto the towel to drain off the access oil.

Serve immediately with dipping sauces, some freshly chopped

parsley, lemon zest and lemons.

Let the oil cool and then pour it into the same bottle you got it

out of, close it with a lid tightly and dispose of it with the rest of

your garbage.

13. Fried rice

INGREDIENTS

- 3 tablespoons butter, divided

- 2 eggs, whisked

- 2 medium carrots, peeled and diced

- 1 small white onion, diced

- 1/2 cup frozen peas

- 3 cloves garlic, minced

- salt and black pepper

- 4 cups cooked and chilled rice (I prefer short-grain white rice)

- 3 green onions, thinly sliced

- 3–4 tablespoons soy sauce, or more to taste

- 2 teaspoons oyster sauce (optional)

- 1/2 teaspoons toasted sesame oil

INSTRUCTIONS

Heat 1/2 tablespoon of butter in a large sauté pan* over medium-high heat until melted. Add egg, and cook until scrambled, stirring occasionally. Remove egg, and transfer to a separate plate.

Add an additional 1 tablespoon butter to the pan and heat until melted. Add carrots, onion, peas and garlic, and season with a generous pinch of salt and pepper. Sauté for about 5 minutes or until the onion and carrots are soft. Increase heat to high, add in the remaining 1 1/2 tablespoons of butter, and stir until melted. Immediately add the rice, green onions, soy sauce and oyster sauce (if using), and stir until combined. Continue sautéing for an additional 3 minutes to fry the rice, stirring occasionally. (I like to let the rice rest for a bit between stirs so that it can crisp

up on the bottom.) Then add in the eggs and stir to combine.

Remove from heat, and stir in the sesame oil until combined.

Taste and season with extra soy sauce, if needed.

Serve immediately, or refrigerate in a sealed container for up to

3 days.

14. Simple turmeric rice with peas

INGREDIENTS

- 1 cup basmati rice

- 1 cup vegetable or chicken stock

- 1 cup water

- 2 Tbs unsalted butter

- 1 tsp turmeric

- 1 tsp kosher salt

- 1 cup frozen peas thawed

- 1 Tbs fresh parsley chopped

INSTRUCTIONS

In a large saucepan, bring the stock and water to a boil. Put the rice in a strainer and rinse with water for 30 seconds.

Add the rice to the boiling stock and water along with the butter, turmeric, and salt. Cover and reduce heat to low. Cook 18-20 minutes until water is absorbed. Remove from the heat.

Add the peas in a layer over the rice, cover, and let them steam to heat 5 minutes. Toss the peas in with the rice and taste for seasoning. Garnish with fresh parsley.

15. Texas Hash

INGREDIENTS

- 2 tablespoons olive oil

- 1 cup diced onion

- 1 cup diced green bell pepper

- 1 tablespoon minced fresh garlic

- 1 pound ground beef

- 1/2 teaspoon dry mustard

- 2 1/2 teaspoons chili powder

- 2 teaspoons salt

- 1/4 teaspoon freshly ground black pepper

- 1/2 cup uncooked long grain white rice

- 2 tablespoons tomato paste

- 1 14.5-ounce can diced tomatoes with juice

- 1 cup water

- 1 1/2 teaspoons Worcestershire sauce

- Grated cheddar or Monterey jack cheese (optional)

PREPARATION

Add onion, peppers, garlic, ground beef, dry mustard, chili powder, salt and pepper in a skillet with olive oil. Sauté until ground beef is browned and stirring as it cooks to ensure beef is broken up.

Add rice and tomato paste and cook for 3 minutes.

Add canned tomatoes and juice, water, and Worcestershire sauce. Simmer for 20 minutes, covered.

Remove lid after 20 minutes and fluff with fork. If mixture is

soupy or wet cook for an additional 2 minutes uncovered.

Sprinkle with grated cheese if desired.

16. Broccoli chicken casserole

INGREDIENTS

- 8 ounces uncooked pasta* (I used whole-wheat rotini)

- 1 large head of broccoli*, cut into bite-sized florets

  (about 1 pound of florets)

- 2 tablespoons butter or olive oil

- 1 small white onion, thinly sliced

- 8 ounces baby bella (cremini) mushrooms, thinly sliced

- 4 cloves garlic, minced

- 3 tablespoons flour

- 1 cup chicken or vegetable stock

- 1 1/2 cups milk

- 1 teaspoon Dijon mustard

- 1/2 teaspoon fine sea salt

- 1/4 teaspoon freshly-cracked black pepper

- 2 cups (8 ounces) shredded sharp cheddar cheese, divided

- 2 cups diced (or shredded) cooked chicken

INSTRUCTIONS

Heat oven to 400°F.

Cook pasta in a large stockpot of generously-salted boiling water until it is al dente. However, about 1 minute before the pasta is done, add the broccoli to the boiling pasta water and stir until combined. Drain both the pasta and broccoli, and set aside.

Meanwhile, heat the butter (or oil) in a large sauté pan over medium-high heat. Add the onion and sauté for 3 minutes, stirring occasionally. Add the mushrooms and garlic and sauté for 5 more minutes, stirring occasionally, or until the mushrooms are cooked through.

Sprinkle the flour evenly over the onion mixture and stir until combined. Cook for 1 minute, stirring occasionally. Add in the stock, and stir everything together until most of the clumps are gone. Add in the milk, Dijon, salt and pepper and stir until combined. Continue cooking the sauce until it reaches a simmer. Then remove from heat and stir in 1 cup of the shredded cheese until it is combined. Taste and season with

additional salt and pepper, if needed.

In a large 9 x 13-inch baking dish, combine the cooked pasta,

broccoli, mushroom sauce and chicken. Toss until combined.

Smooth the casserole out into an even layer.

Bake uncovered for 15 minutes. Then remove pan from the

oven, sprinkle the remaining cheddar cheese evenly on top of

the casserole, and bake for 10 more minutes or until the cheese

is nice and melty.

Serve warm, garnished with extra black pepper and/or fresh

herbs, if desired.

17. Shepherd's pie

SHEPHERD'S PIE INGREDIENTS:

- 1 tablespoon olive oil

- 1.25 pounds ground beef

- 1 medium white onion, peeled and diced

- 8 ounces baby bella or white button mushrooms, finely

  diced

- 2 medium carrots, finely diced

- 2 stalks celery, finely diced

- 4 cloves garlic, peeled and minced

- 1/4 cup all-purpose flour

- 1/2 cup dry red wine (or you can sub in more beef stock

  instead)

- 2 cups beef stock (or vegetable or chicken stock)

- 2 tablespoons tomato paste

- 2 tablespoons Worcestershire sauce

- 2 bay leaves

- 2 sprigs each fresh rosemary and thyme (or whatever herbs you love)

- 1/2 cup frozen peas

- sea salt and freshly-cracked black pepper

- 1 batch mashed potatoes (see below)

MASHED POTATO INGREDIENTS:

- 2.5 pounds potatoes (either Russets, Yukon golds, or a mix of the two)

- 1/4 cup butter

- 1/2 cup whole milk, or more as needed

- 2 ounces cream cheese (or 1/2 cup plain Greek yogurt)

- sea salt and freshly-cracked black pepper

INSTRUCTIONS

Cook the mashed potatoes. Follow the instructions here to prepare a half batch of this mashed potatoes recipe. Once the mashed potatoes are ready to go, remove from heat and set aside until ready to use.

Brown the beef (or lamb). Meanwhile, heat the oil in a large sauté pan over medium-high heat. Add the ground beef (or lamb) and cook until browned, crumbling it with a wooden spoon as it cooks. Transfer the cooked beef to a separate plate with a wooden spoon and set aside, reserving any grease in the sauté pan that it has left behind. (Or if there is no leftover grease, add an extra tablespoon of oil to the pan.)

Sauté the veggies. Add the onion and sauté for 5 minutes, stirring occasionally. Add the carrots, celery, mushrooms, garlic and sauté for 5-7 more minutes, stirring occasionally, until softened.

Add in the flour and wine. Stir the flour in with the veggie mixture until evenly combined, then continue to sauté for 1 minute more, stirring frequently. Stir in the wine, then use a wooden spoon to scrape up any browned bits that are stuck to the bottom of the pan.

Add the remaining sauce ingredients. Immediately stir in the stock, tomato paste, Worcestershire sauce, bay leaf, herb sprigs and frozen peas until combined. Continue cooking until the mixture reaches a simmer. Then reduce heat to medium-low to maintain a low simmer, and continue cooking for 5 more minutes, stirring occasionally. Remove and discard the bay leaves and herb sprigs. Stir in the cooked meat Taste and season the mixture with salt and pepper as needed.

Layer it all up. Transfer the filling mixture to a 9 x 13-inch baking dish and spread it out in an even layer. Spoon the mashed potatoes on top and carefully spread them out in an even layer as well.

Bake. Bake uncovered at 400°F for about 20 minutes, or until the potatoes are lightly golden and the filling has started to bubble up around the edges. (If you would like the potatoes to be a bit more browned, you can turn on the broiler for 1 or 2

extra minutes, keeping a close eye on the potatoes so that they

do not burn.)

Garnish and serve. Remove the baking dish from the oven,

sprinkle a few extra herbs on top if you would like, then dish up

your servings while the shepherd's pie is still nice and warm. Or

store the pie in sealed containers in the refrigerator for up to 3

days, or freeze for up to 3 months.

18. Baked ravioli

Ingredients

- 1 tablespoon extra virgin olive oil

- 1 medium onion, chopped (about 1 cup chopped)

- 3 garlic cloves, minced

- Salt and pepper

- 1 can (28-oz) whole tomatoes

- 1 can (28-oz) fire-roasted crushed tomatoes

- 1 teaspoon dried oregano

- 1/2 teaspoon dried thyme

- 2 lbs frozen cheese ravioli

- 1 1/2 cups shredded mozzarella

- 1/2 cup grated parmesan

- Chopped parsley or basil, for garnish

Instructions

Heat the olive oil in a large skillet over medium heat. Add the

onion and cook, stirring occasionally until softened, about 5 minutes. Add the garlic and cook an additional 30 seconds then season with salt and pepper.

Add the whole tomatoes and the crushed tomatoes. Season with the oregano and thyme.

Bring the mixture to a boil, then reduce the heat and simmer, breaking up the tomatoes as it cooks. Cook until the sauce is thickened and reduced, about 20-25 minutes.

Preheat the oven to 425ºF. Spray a 9×13-inch baking dish with nonstick cooking spray.

Meanwhile, bring a large pot of salted water to a boil. Add the ravioli and cook according to the package directions. Drain and return to the pot.

When the sauce is thickened, taste for seasoning and add more

salt and pepper, if needed.

Add the sauce to the pasta and gently toss to combine.

Pour the pasta and sauce into the prepared baking dish.

Sprinkle with both cheeses.

Bake until the cheese is melted and golden, about 20 minutes.

Let the pasta sit for a few minutes before serving. Top with

chopped parsley or basil, if desired.

19. Creamy chicken soup

Ingredients

For the Roux:

- 2 tablespoons oil

- 2 tablespoons unsalted butter

- 4 tablespoons all-purpose flour

- cup reduced-salt chicken stock

- For the Soup:

- 2 tablespoons unsalted butter

- 2 tablespoons oil

- 4-6 carrots peeled and cut into 1/8" slices

- 2 celery stalks cut into 1/8" slices

- 1 medium yellow onion diced

- 1 garlic clove minced

- 3 cups reduced-salt chicken broth

- ¼ cup dry or semi-dry white wine; a good drinking wine

- 3½ cups milk cream or half and half (or a mixture of cream and skim milk)

- 2 tablespoons chicken base granules or chicken cubes

- ½ teaspoon freshly cracked black pepper

- 1 tablespoon dried parsley or 2 tablespoons minced fresh parsley

- 3 dried bay leaves

- 1½ teaspoon Herbs de Provence

- 1/2 teaspoon turmeric optional

- ½ teaspoon paprika optional

- ¼ teaspoon red pepper flakes optional

- 4-5 cups cooked chicken cubed or shredded – rotisserie chicken works well, but do NOT use smoked chicken.

- Garnish: Shredded Gruyere cheese

- Chopped fresh parsley

Instructions

For the Roux:

Heat 2 tablespoons oil and 2 tablespoons butter in a medium saucepan then sprinkle the flour on top. Whisk quickly until well combined. Cook, whisking occasionally, until the roux turns light golden brown. Slowly, while whisking, add 1-cup chicken broth to the roux and whisk vigorously until smooth. Remove the roux from the heat and set it aside while combining other ingredients.

For the Soup:

In a large Dutch oven, heat 2 tablespoons butter and 2 tablespoons oil over MED-HIGH heat. Add the carrots and celery, sauté 5 minutes; stir occasionally. Add the diced onions and cook 3 additional minutes or until the onions are translucent. Add the minced garlic and cook 30 seconds just long enough for the garlic to bloom.

Slowly add 1 cup of broth while scraping the bottom of the pot to deglaze the pan. Add the rest of the broth and the wine, the roux and stir well. Bring the mixture to a boil and stir often..

Reduce the heat to LOW and add all other ingredients except the garnishes.

Simmer 15 minutes then taste and adjust seasonings, if necessary. This is the time to add salt or pepper, if desired. Continue to simmer the soup until it thickens, about 30-45 minutes more, or to the desired consistency.

Discard the bay leaves.

Garnish with sprinklings of shredded Gruyere and fresh parsley.

Serve with crusty bread. Mmm-Mmm GREAT!

Enjoy!!

20. Slow cooker split pea soup

Ingredients

- 16 oz dried split peas (about 2 cups)

- 1 1/2 lb ham bone

- 3 carrots, diced

- 1 yellow onion, diced

- 1 shallot, diced

- 2 stalks celery, diced

- 3 cloves garlic, minced

- 1 tsp dried thyme

- 1/2 tsp ground black pepper

- 1 bay leaf

- 6 cups low sodium chicken stock

Instructions

In the bowl of a slow cooker, combine the split peas, carrots, yellow onion, shallot, celery, garlic, thyme, pepper, bay leaf, and chicken stock. Mix well.

Add the ham bone on top and nestle into the contents of the slow cooker.

Cover and cook on Low for 5-6 hours, or until ham is tender and easily pulls off the bone.

Remove the ham and shred into bite-size pieces using two forks, then return the ham meat to the slow cooker, and discard the bone.

Remove the bay leaf and serve.

21. Roasted garlic soup

Ingredients

- 2 tablespoons extra virgin olive oil, divided

- 2 large heads hardneck garlic (12 − 15 cloves each), divided

- 1 large shallot, peeled and sliced

- 1/2 sea salt, divided, plus more as needed

- 1/4 teaspoon chili pepper flakes

- Black pepper to taste

- 1 tablespoon white wine

- 4 - 5 cups rich broth (chicken or vegetable)

- 4 sprigs each fresh thyme and parsley, tied with twine

- 2 medium russet potatoes, cut into 1-inch cubes

Instructions

Preheat oven to 400 degrees F.

Trim root end off one head of garlic. Set cloves, trimmed side down, in a small, oven-proof ramekin. Add 1 tablespoon olive oil and a pinch sea salt. Cover with foil, set on a rimmed baking sheet, and slide into oven. Roast garlic about 15 minutes, or until garlic is soft, but not at all brown. Once garlic is done, carefully remove foil and set aside to cool. When cool enough to handle, slide cloves out of their skins and reserve. Reserve garlic-infused olive oil.

Meanwhile, trim, smash, and peel remaining head of garlic. In a heavy bottomed 2- or 3-quart pot, 1 tablespoon olive oil over medium heat. Add cloves to pot, along with the sliced shallots, a generous pinch sea salt, chili flakes, and several twists black

pepper. Sauté 2 - 3 minutes, then turn heat to low, cover the

pot, and cook until garlic and shallots are transluscent and

fragrant, about 20 minutes.

Next, turn heat to medium, add white wine, scrape up any

brown bits, then pour in 3 cups stock. Add potatoes, reserved

roasted garlic cloves and olive oil, and tied herbs (or bouquet

garni), along with a 1/2 teaspoon sea salt.

Bring mixture to a boil, and then turn heat down to a bubbling

simmer. Cook until potatoes are tender, about 15 minutes.

Remove bouquet garni and carefully puree soup in a blender.

Return soup to pot, adding up to 1 - 2 more cups of broth,

depending on your preferred texture. Add sea salt to taste, add a splash more white wine if needed, lots and lots of black pepper, and serve topped with minced thyme and parsley leaves.

The flavor will develop further after a day in the fridge. The soup reheats beautifully, but does tend to thicken keep a 1/2 cup of stock (water will work, too) on hand to thin soup if needed.

Helpful tips for people on soft diets

Although consuming a diet comprising of just delicate foods can be troublesome, the following tips may make following such an eating regimen easier:

Choose healthy choices. While soft, sugar-laden food varieties like cakes and pastries may seem appealing, ensuring you're devouring healthy foods like vegetables, natural products, and proteins is best for your wellbeing. Pick a variety of supplement rich food varieties.

Season your food. Using spices and other mild seasonings can help make food more palatable.

Focus on protein. Adding protein to each feast and snack is especially significant for people recuperating from surgery and those who are malnourished.

Eat little, predictable meals. Rather than consuming large suppers, it's prescribed to consume multiple little dinners over the course of the day when following a soft diet.

Eat gradually and chew thoroughly. Taking your time while eating and chewing food thoroughly is significant for many people on soft diets, including those recuperating from abdominal medical procedure and with neurological conditions.

Sit upright and take small sips of liquid between bites.

Plan meals ahead of time. Finding meals that work with a mechanical soft diet can be difficult. Planning suppers ahead of time can help lessen stress and make mealtime simpler.

Keep appliances helpful. Blenders, sifters, and food processors can be used to make delicious, soft-diet-approved plans. Typically, soft diets are used as transitional diets for short periods until a person is prepared to begin eating a customary consistency diet once more. Your medical services provider will give you Instructions on how lengthy you should follow a delicate food diet, while a registered dietitian can furnish you with any other appropriate information. In the event that you have any inquiries or concerns about following a delicate food diet or how to change back to a regular-consistency diet, ask your medical provider for advice.

Different Tips for a Soft Food Diet

On the off chance that your doctor puts you on a soft food diet, ask them to help you make sure that you're getting enough nutrition. Each day, you need to be eating:

- 2 servings of protein

- 2 servings of dairy

- 5 servings of fruits and vegetables

- Aim to drink 8-10 glasses of water or fluid, as well.

At supper time, sit as upright as you can during the meal and for the half-hour afterward. Don't race through your meal. Take the time to appreciate it without distractions. If you have inconvenience gulping or the food gets stuck in your throat, check in with your doctor.

Conclusion

Healthcare suppliers regularly prescribe soft food diets to help people recover from medical procedure and disease and make biting and digesting food easier. When following a soft food diet, it's vital to choose soft, effectively absorbable foods and avoid food varieties that are hard to bite or digest. Spicy and potentially aggravating foods ought to similarly be kept away from. Albeit a delicate food diet can be troublesome to follow, it's utilized to promote recuperation, so it's significant to follow your healthcare supplier's instructions and comply until you're ready to change back to a regular diet.